Counting in 10s

Purses

Draw the correct number of 10p coins in each purse to match its label.

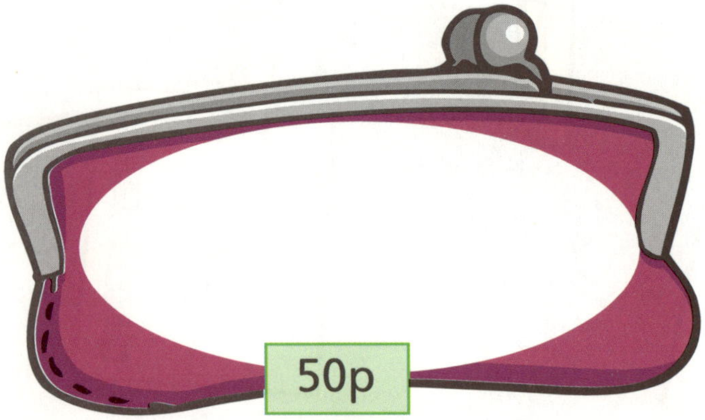

50p

20p

70p

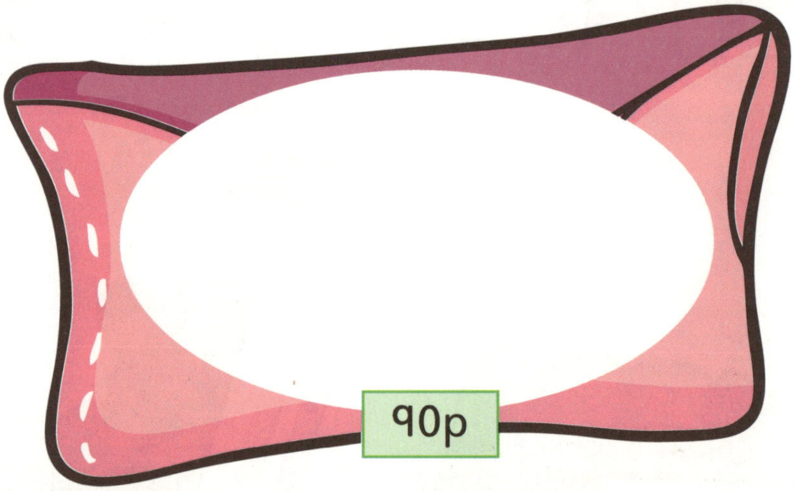

90p

30p

100p

eXtra Choose any two purses. Imagine you are putting the two sets of coins into one big purse. How much is in the big purse? Draw the purse and all the coins, and label it.

Parcel post

Place value
A1

Draw 10p and 1p stamps on the parcels to match the labels.

12p

16p

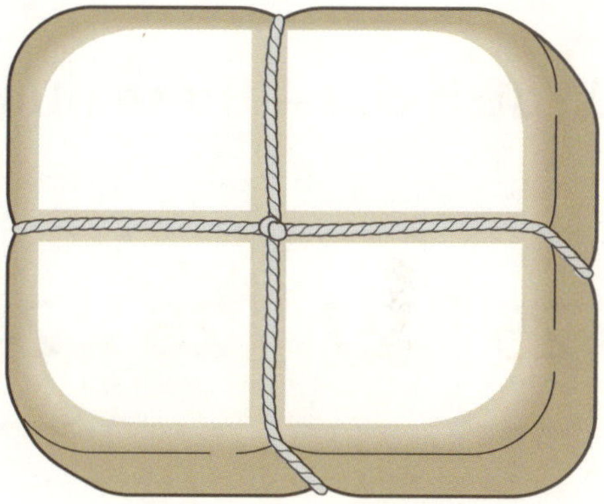

23p

21p

15p

31p

 **A parcel needs 24p in stamps. You can use stamps with values of 1p, 2p, 5p and 10p. How many different ways could you make a total value of 24p?**

A1 Place value and ordering

Biggest, smallest

For each set of cards, colour the biggest number **red** and the smallest number **blue**.

| 9 | 10 | 11 | | 15 | 14 | 13 | | 19 | 18 | 17 |

Watch out – these number cards are not in order!

| 25 | 27 | 26 | 24 | | 14 | 13 | 11 | 12 |

| 18 | 19 | 17 | 16 | | 31 | 32 | 38 | 36 |

| 27 | 18 | 12 | 24 | 21 | | 35 | 39 | 41 | 47 | 33 |

| 34 | 35 | 44 | 24 | 25 |

How did you find the biggest numbers?

eXtra Make up your own set of cards. You choose how many cards and which numbers to use. Shuffle them and give them to a partner. Ask your partner to find the biggest number and the smallest number.

Hop, skip and jump

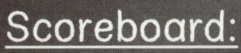
Addition
B1

It is sports day.
Leah, Otis and Chen are in the jumping competition. They each do three types of jump: hop, skip or jump.

Scoreboard:
One hop = 2 points
One skip = 3 points
One jump = 4 points

Leah does one hop, one skip, and one jump. She scores 2 + 3 + 4. Her total is 9.

	Scores	Total
Leah	2 + 3 + 4	9
Otis		
Chen		
Winner:		

Otis does two skips and one jump. Write his score in the table.

Chen does one jump, one skip and one hop. Write his score in the table.

Who has the most points? Write their name in the table.

 **eXtra** What is the highest possible score? What is the lowest possible score? How many different scores can be made?

 Addition

Cube scores

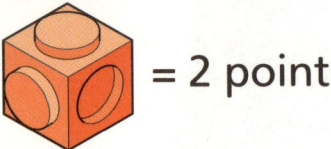 = 2 points 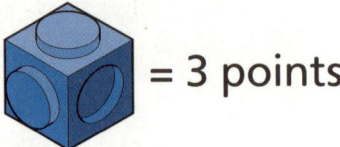 = 3 points 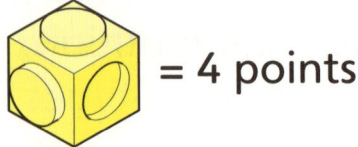 = 4 points

Throw two dice.
Find the total.

How many different ways can you make your total?
You can use any three cubes.
Write all the additions.
Play three games.

> Can you use a system to find all the different ways?

Total:	Total:	Total:

eXtra — How many different totals can you make using four cubes?

Totals of 7

Addition B1

Bag 1

Bag 2

Write a number from the first bag.

What number from the second bag would you need to add to make a total of 7?

Write another way to make 7.

How many different ways are there?

How many different ways are there if you can only use each number once?

What do you notice?

eXtra How many ways can you make 7 using pairs of numbers between 0 and 10, and using addition and subtraction?

 Length

Measuring in hands

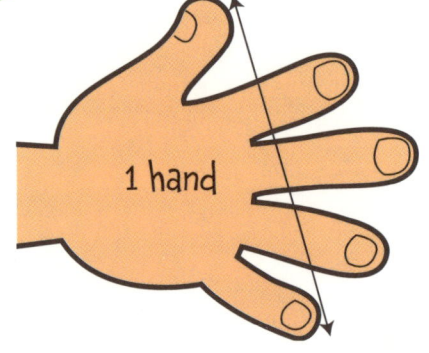

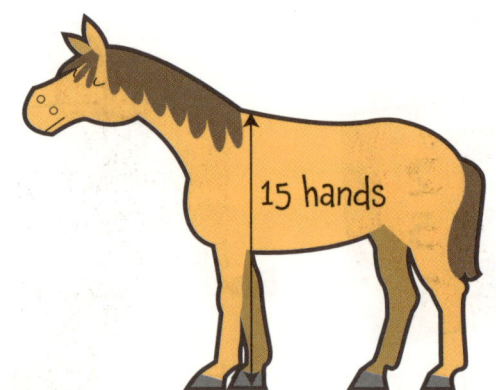

Find real objects like the ones in the picture. Estimate their height in hands. Measure their heights using your hands. Write the number of hands in the boxes.

Compare your answers with a partner. Are they the same?

What could you measure with instead?

 A 15-hand horse is 60 inches tall. How big is each hand?

How many feet?

Length C1

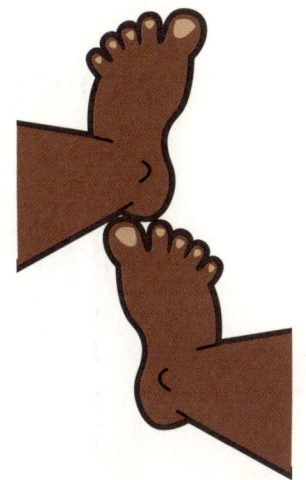

How long is the classroom in feet?

How wide is the classroom in feet?

I estimate the classroom is as long as _____ of my feet.

I estimate the classroom is as wide as _____ of my feet.

What things do you need to be careful of when you measure using your feet?

The classroom is as long as _____ of my feet.

The classroom is as wide as _____ of my feet.

Did you get the same answers as your partner?

 **Measure the length and width of the classroom using a ruler marked in feet. Do you get the same answers as earlier? Why?**

Time
C1

Days of the week

Play the days-of-the-week ladder game with a partner.

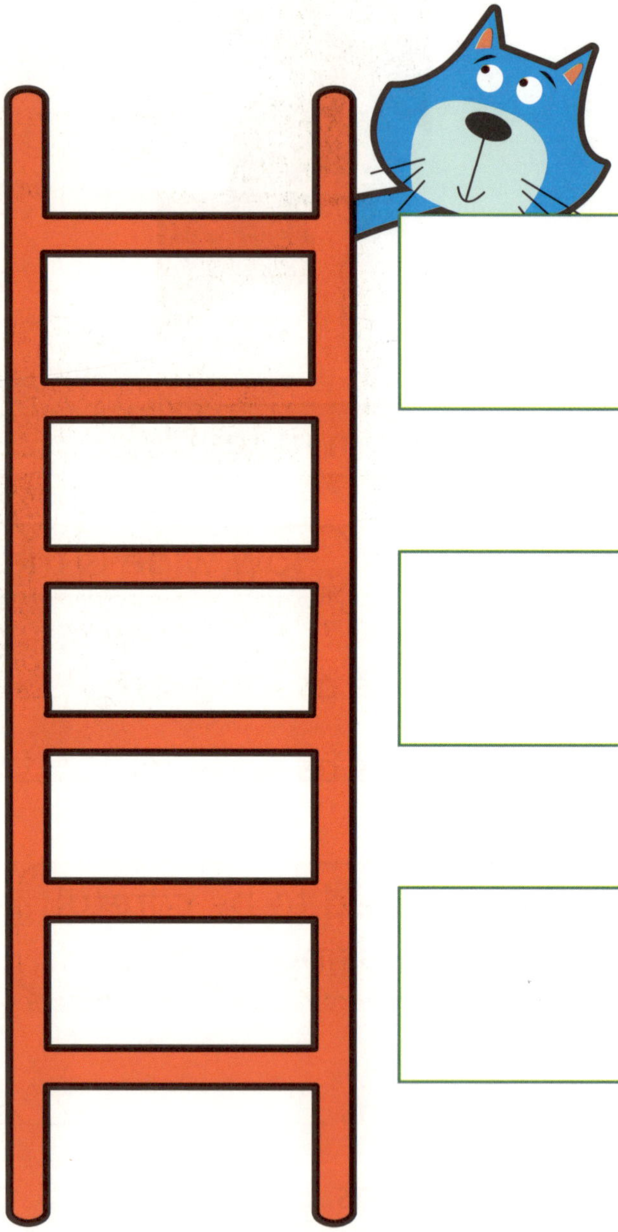

Then write the days of the week on the ladder.
In the boxes draw something you usually do on each day.

Make up a rhyme or a song to help other children remember the days of the week in order.

Where are the shapes?

2D shape
D1

Look at this building:

Can you see any rectangles? How many can you see?

Can you see any squares? How many can you see?

I can see ☐ rectangles. I can see ☐ squares.

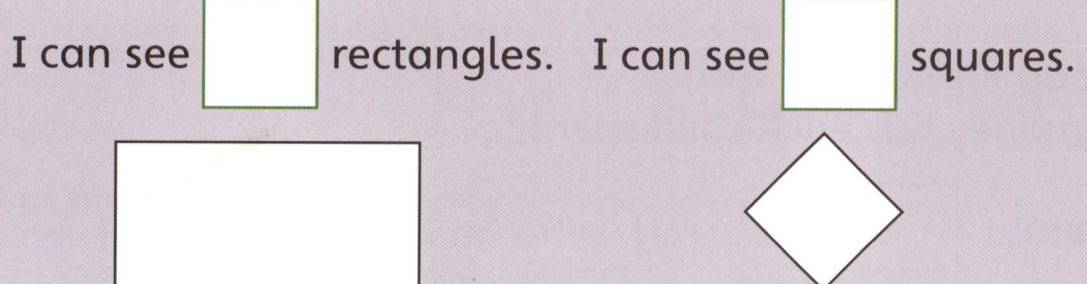

Did your partner count the same number of shapes?

Cut out pictures of different shapes from magazines. Sort them into groups. Make labels to name the groups.

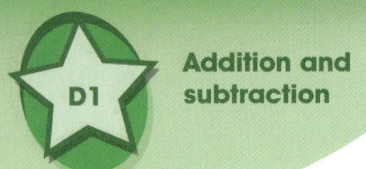

Addition and subtraction

Money banks

Jane  Tom  Isaac

Jane has 10p in her money bank.
Tom has 1p less than Jane.
Isaac has 1p less than Tom.

Draw lines to join the children to their money banks.

Each child had 10p to start with.
How much money has each child spent?

Jane has spent ☐ p

Tom has spent ☐ p

Isaac has spent ☐ p

Who has spent the most?

Who has spent the least?

eXtra Tell a story to a friend that explains what the children spent their money on.

Granny's knitting

Granny is knitting. There are two stitches on the first row.

On the second row Granny doubles the number of stitches.

Doubling E1

Every time Granny starts a new row she doubles the number of stitches.

Complete the table.

	Number of stitches
Row 1	2
Row 2	
Row 3	
Row 4	
Row 5	

On one row Granny drops half the stitches by mistake. There are 16 stitches left on each needle.

How many stitches are there on this row? _____

How many stitches should there be? _____

Which number row is Granny knitting? _____

 How many stitches would there be on row 6? How many on row 10? How do you know? Can you make up a rule for this?

Doubling E1

Double-buttoned coat

Finn has made a new coat.
He has not sewn on all the buttons.
Draw the missing buttons.

How many buttons are there now? _____

Draw some different numbers of buttons on these coats.
There must always be the same number on each side.

_____ buttons   _____ buttons   _____ buttons

Finn decides to put 24 buttons on his coat.
How many buttons are on each side? _____

Finn puts two rows of buttons on the back
of the coat to match the ones on the front.
How many buttons are there altogether? _____

 Finn has made some more coats. They all have the same number of buttons. There are 48 buttons altogether. How many coats could there be? How many buttons could be on each coat?

What did she buy?

Money
E1

Mrs Button spent 50p. What might she have bought?

> Compare your answer with someone else's. What do you notice?

Find some more ways Mrs Button might have spent 50p.

> How many different ways do you think there are?

 **All the items in the shop have been reduced by 1p. How much money does Mrs Button save if she buys the same items as before?**

Counting A2

Number words

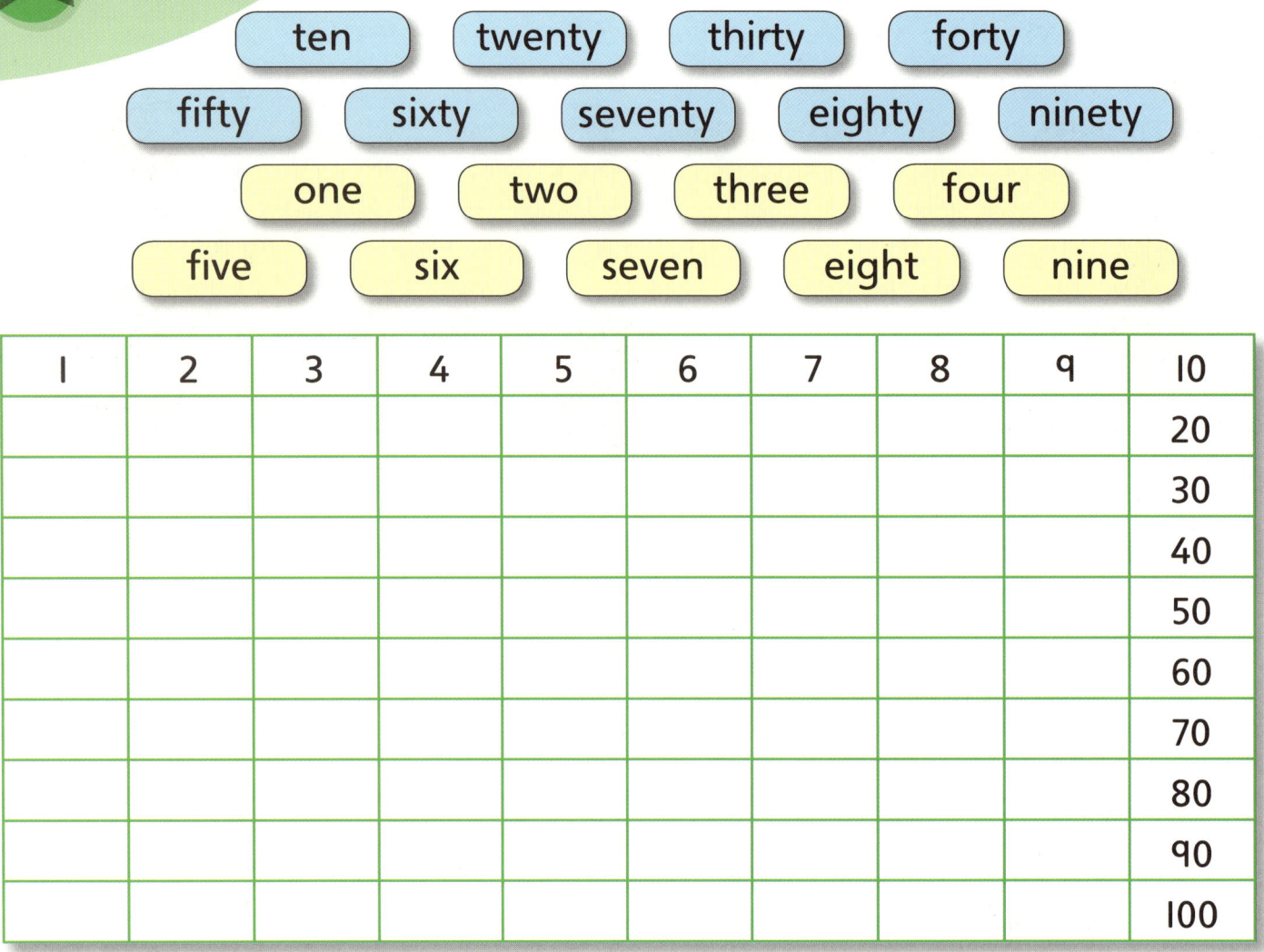

Complete the grid. Then write each number below in words.
Use the matching colour to shade each number on the grid.

37 _____   64 _____

83 _____   21 _____

42 _____   55 _____

78 _____   96 _____

eXtra: Which 2-digit numbers written in words will have the most letters? Why? Check to see if you are right. What about the number with fewest letters?

Counting in 10s

The three shaded numbers are the start of a sequence.
The sequence starts at 5 and counts on in 10s.
Shade the rest of the numbers in the sequence.

9	19	2	30	90	1	74	60	100	6
99	29	39	12	54	64	11	84	16	80
89	79	49	44	22	21	97	26	94	93
98	69	59	32		31		77	36	83
88	78	42	24	14		50	67	73	46
20	68	10	52		4		57	56	63
48	58	62	45	55	61	37	66	43	53
38	25	35	72	65	27	71	40	76	33
15	28	82	85	75	81	17	13	23	86
5	18	8	92	95	91	3	7	96	70

There are eight more sequences like this.
Can you find them?
Use a different colour for each sequence.

Fill in the missing numbers in the middle of the grid.

**Which numbers are not coloured? Why do you think that is?
Pick a sequence and write it out in words.**

Counting

10 more, 10 less

Fill in the missing numbers. Each number is 10 more or 10 less than the middle number.

146

139

287

613

352

287

431

578

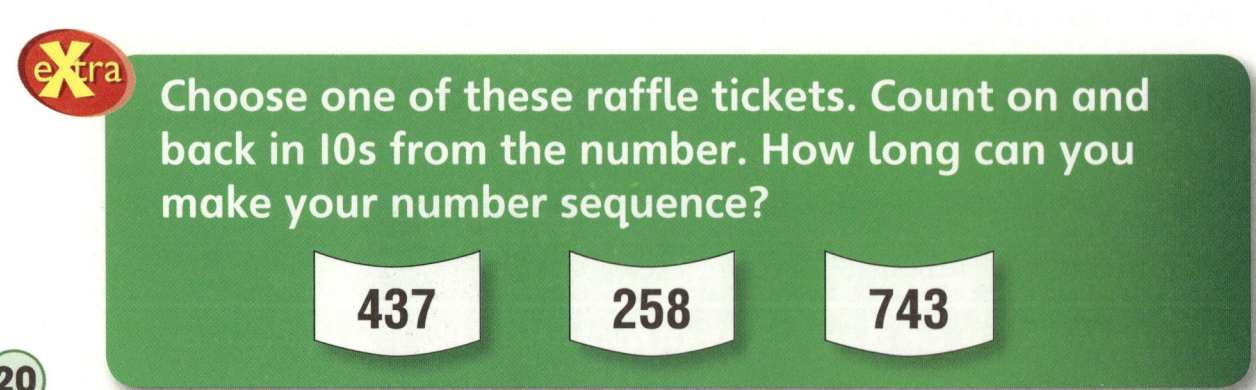

Choose one of these raffle tickets. Count on and back in 10s from the number. How long can you make your number sequence?

437   258   743

Colouring to order

Use the order cards from PCM 22 and a colour-spot dice to find out how to colour each stripe on the scarf.

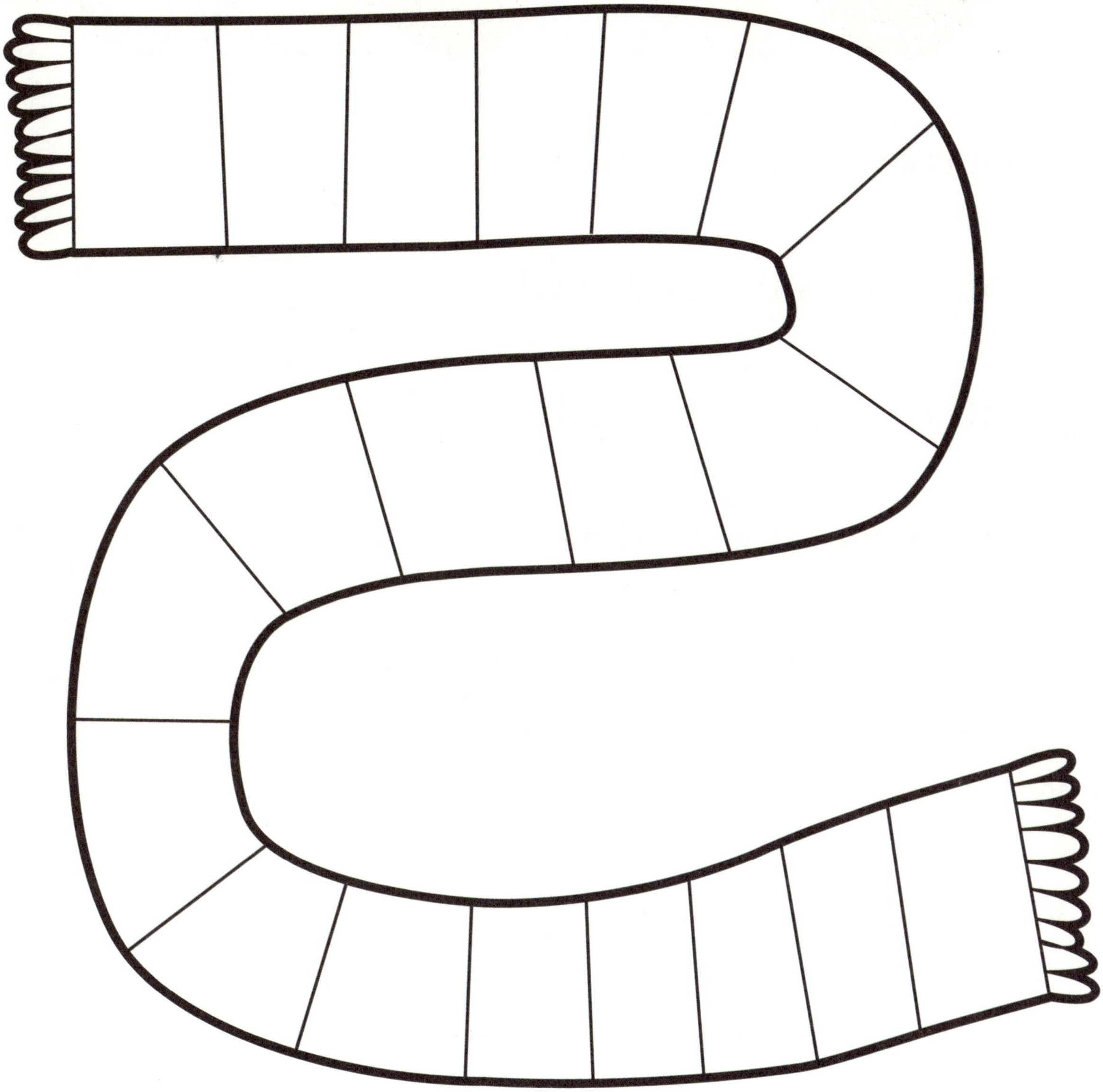

Ordering A2

The winner is the first person to finish colouring their scarf.

 **Can you answer these order questions?**
- What is the 12th letter of the alphabet?
- What is the 3rd letter in your name?
- What is the 4th odd number?
- What is the 17th letter of the alphabet?

Make up some questions like this for a partner to answer.

A2 Ordering

Beads

What colour is the 2nd bead?

What colour is the 4th bead?

What colour is the 1st bead?

What colour is the third bead?

What colour would the seventh bead be?

What colour would the ninth bead be?

What colour would the 10th bead be?

What colour would the 8th bead be?

What colour would the 12th bead be?

What colour would the 15th bead be?

 Now make up your own bead pattern. Show a partner and take turns to ask and answer questions about each other's beads.

Between

1	2	3	4	5	6	7	8	9	10
11	12	13	14	15	16	17	18	19	20
21	22	23	24	25	26	27	28	29	30
31	32	33	34	35	36	37	38	39	40
41	42	43	44	45	46	47	48	49	50
51	52	53	54	55	56	57	58	59	60
61	62	63	64	65	66	67	68	69	70
71	72	73	74	75	76	77	78	79	80
81	82	83	84	85	86	87	88	89	90
91	92	93	94	95	96	97	98	99	100

Ordering A2

Colour the numbers between 4 and 7 **red**.

Colour the numbers between 83 and 88 **blue**.

Colour the numbers between 15 and 19 **green**.

Colour the numbers between 44 and 57 **purple**.

Colour the numbers between 29 and 34 **orange**.

Colour the numbers between 68 and 75 **yellow**.

eXtra

Put a tick in the box if the sentence is true.
Put a cross in the box if the sentence is false.

- ☐ There are seven numbers between 1 and 7.
- ☐ There are five numbers between 70 and 76.
- ☐ 74 is half-way between 70 and 80.

Write some true/false sentences for a partner.

Position B2

What's my number?

"My number is beside a yellow square and above the frog."

Shuffle the cards from PCM 26.
Put them face down.
Take turns to pick a card.
Do not show it to your partner!
Describe the position of your number on this grid.
You must not say the number itself.

Here are some words to help you.

above   below   beside   left   right

10		12	13	🐟
🎈	26	🎁	28	15
24	33	34		16
23	☂️	31	30	🐸
🌼	21	20	🐞	18

eXtra There are numbers hidden under the pictures. Can you work out which numbers they are?

Turning around

Do these parts of your body turn?
Tick the boxes if you think they do.

Position B2

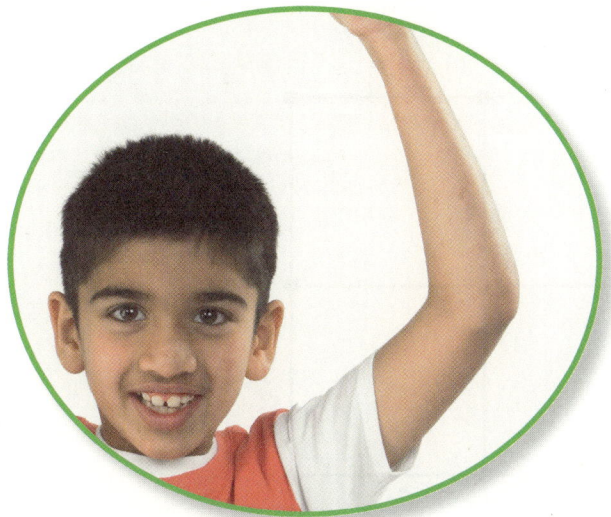

☐ My elbow turns.

☐ My knee turns.

☐ My fingers turn.

☐ My head turns.

Do other people in your group think the same as you?

Give a partner instructions for moving around the room, for example:
Move forward two steps, turn one half turn.

25

Obstacle course

Position B2

Mrs Devi has set up an obstacle course.

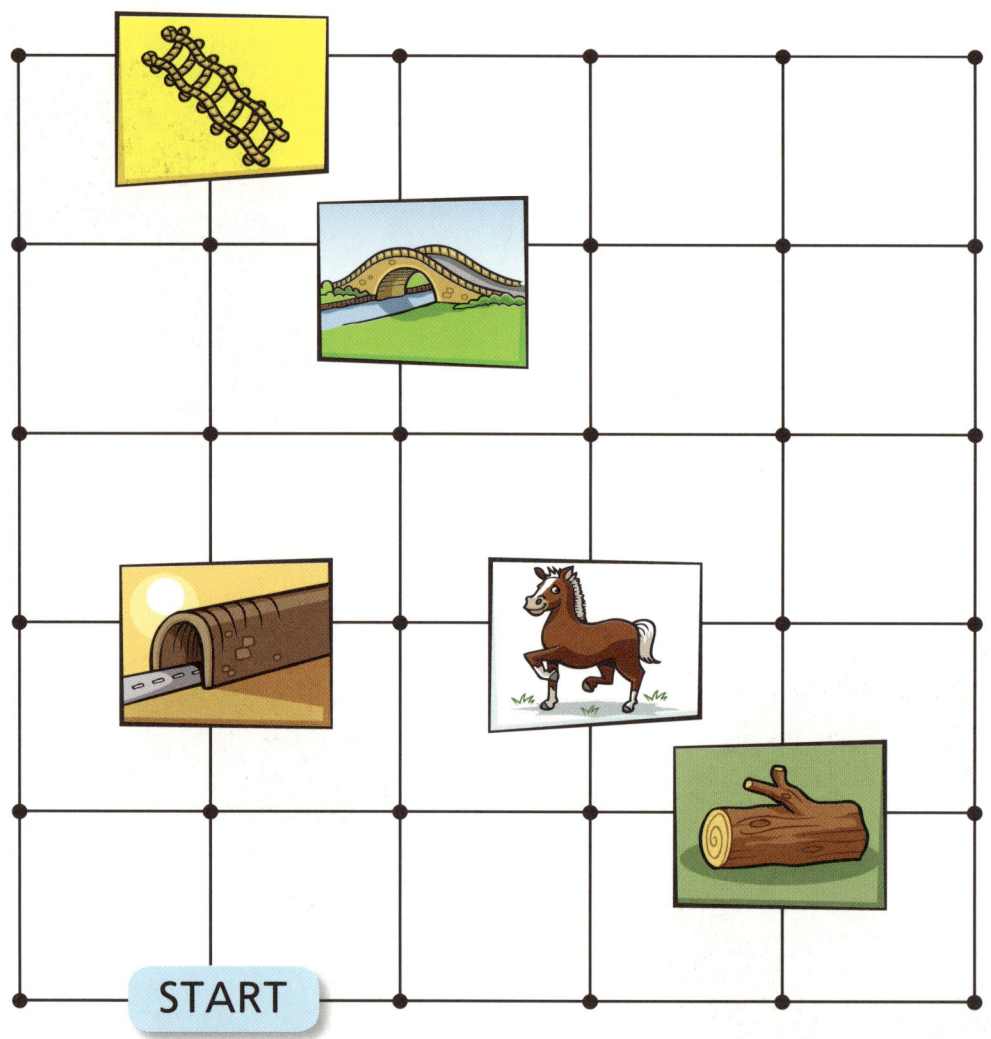

You must visit each obstacle.
You can choose any route, but you must stay on the lines.
Each move between two black dots is one step.

What is the smallest number of steps you could take?
Mark your route. Describe your route to a partner.
Mark your partner's route on your grid in another colour.

eXtra

Write instructions for a route through the blank grid on PCM 28. Challenge a partner to draw the route.

How much is a kilogram?

How many of each item weigh 1 kg?
Guess first, then measure.

estimate ☐

actual ☐

estimate ☐

actual ☐

estimate ☐

actual ☐

estimate ☐

actual ☐

> Which item is lightest? Which is heaviest? How do you know?

 **Find five items in the classroom that you would weigh in kilograms. How much do you think each one weighs? Weigh them to find out.**

Weight C2

Weight C2

How much is a gram?

How many of each item weigh 1g?
Guess first, then measure.

estimate ☐   estimate ☐

actual ☐   actual ☐

estimate ☐   estimate ☐

actual ☐   actual ☐

Which item is lightest? Which is heaviest? How do you know?

Find five items in the classroom that you would weigh in grams. How much do you think each one weighs? Weigh them to find out.

Favourite colours

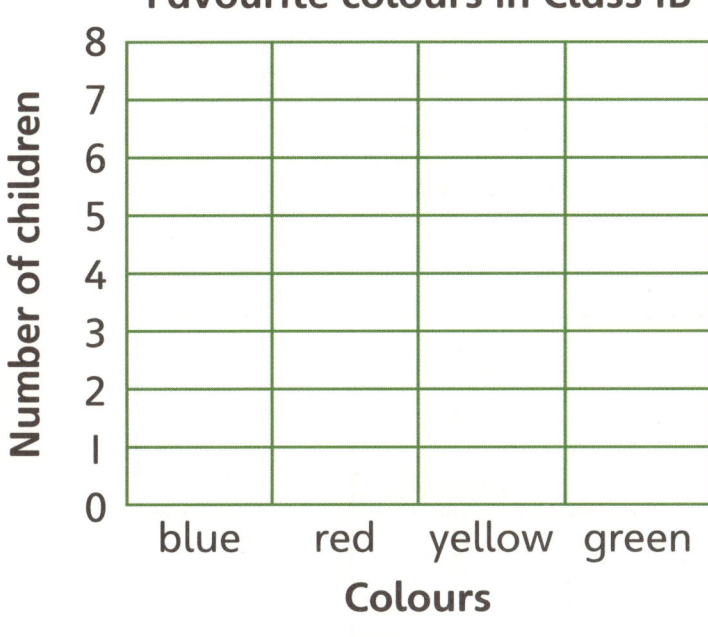

How many like red best? ☐

How many like green best? ☐

☐ is the most popular colour.

☐ is the least popular colour.

 **Make up some questions about the graph. Ask a partner to answer them. Do you agree on the answers?**

Shape D2

Spot the 3D shapes

Choose a counter and put it on 'Start'. With a partner, take turns to throw a dice and move that number of places. If you land on a 3D shape and name it correctly, collect one interlocking cube. The first player to land on the shape robot is the winner.

Now make a 3D model using your interlocking cubes.
Do not show it to your partner! Describe it.
Can your partner make a shape to match your description?

Play the game again. This time, keep going around the track until one person is able to make a bigger cube out of their interlocking cubes.

The shape sorter

Choose a shape. Answer the questions and follow the arrows.

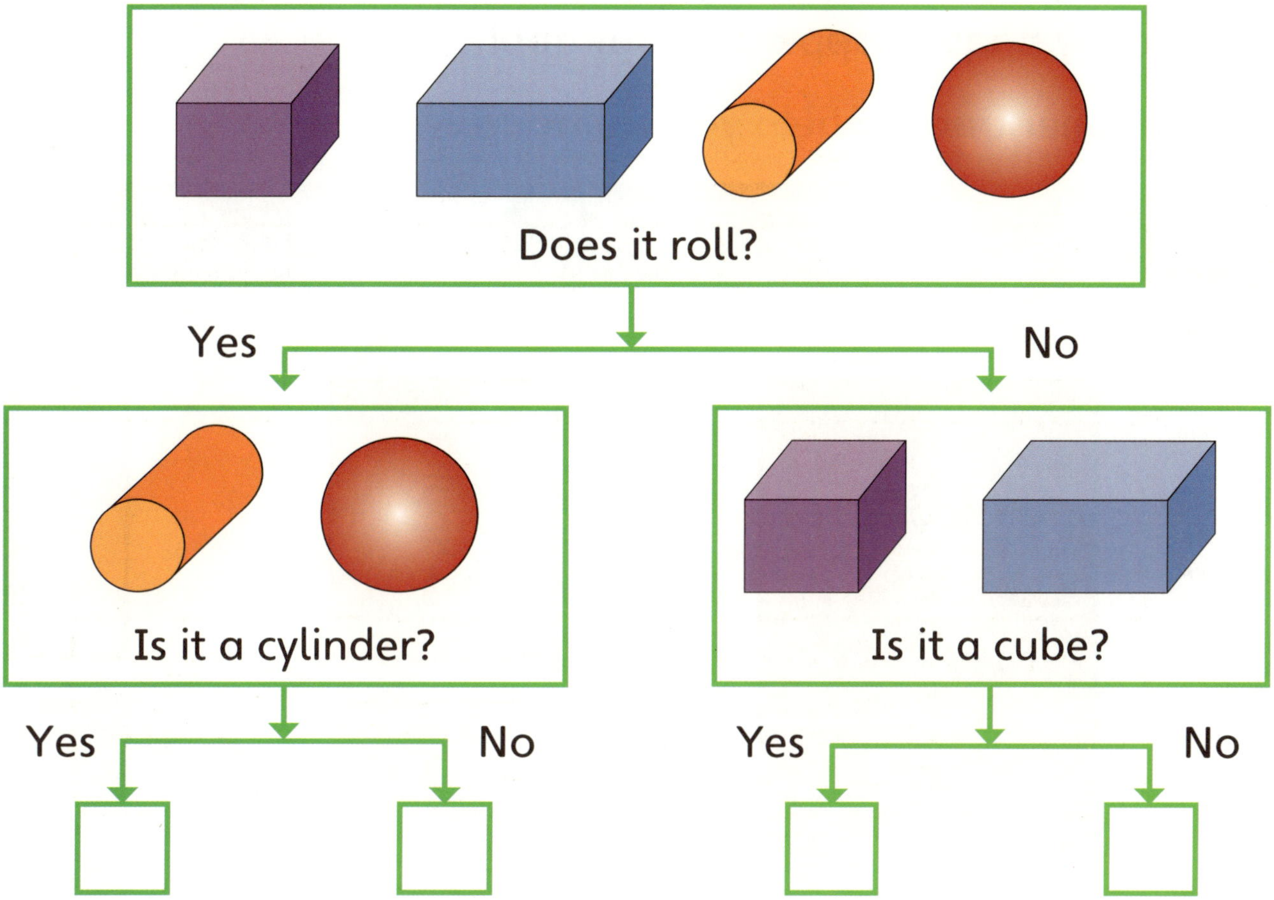

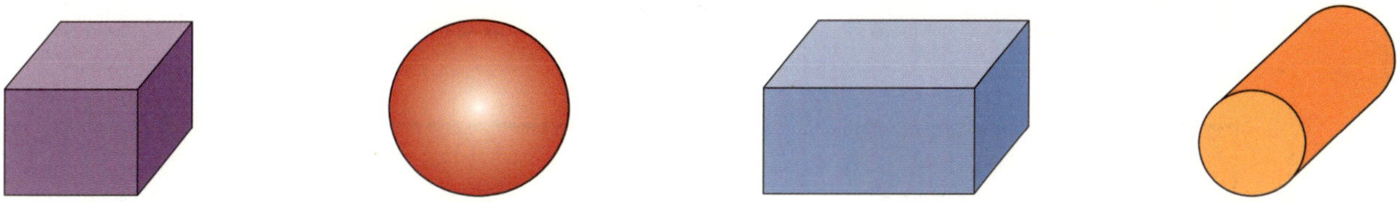

Shape D2

Does it roll?

Yes → **Is it a cylinder?** → Yes ☐ / No ☐

No → **Is it a cube?** → Yes ☐ / No ☐

cube   sphere   cuboid   cylinder

Draw lines to join the shapes to the empty boxes.

Why did you put them in those boxes?

Compare your answers with someone else's.

eXtra

Use the shape sorter to sort a dice, a matchbox, a ball and a glue stick. Which goes where?

Counting

Apple packing

Take a number card. How many groups of 10 are in that number? Put that many bags of apples in your apple box.

Use the number track to help you count up.

10 20 30 40 50 60 70 80 90 100

Who will be first to get 100 apples?

Player 2's apple box

Player 1's apple box

10 apples 10 apples
10 apples 10 apples
10 apples 10 apples
10 apples 10 apples

Counting D2

 **Play again, but take apples from your apple box and put them back on the squares. Who is first to cover all their squares?**

10 apples	10 apples	10 apples	Player 1: Start here
10 apples	10 apples	10 apples	
10 apples	10 apples	10 apples	Player 1: Start here
10 apples	10 apples	10 apples	

Counting E2

Choosing tracks

- Each place a counter on one of the red numbers.
- Take turns to move your counter one space.
- For each move, work out if the number has changed by + 1, + 10, – 1 or – 10. Record this on PCM 44.
- When you reach 9, choose a track to take. You cannot go back the way you came or take the same track as someone else.
- The game ends when you all reach a different red number.
- Add your scores to find your total score. The player with the largest total score wins. Play again. Let someone else go first.

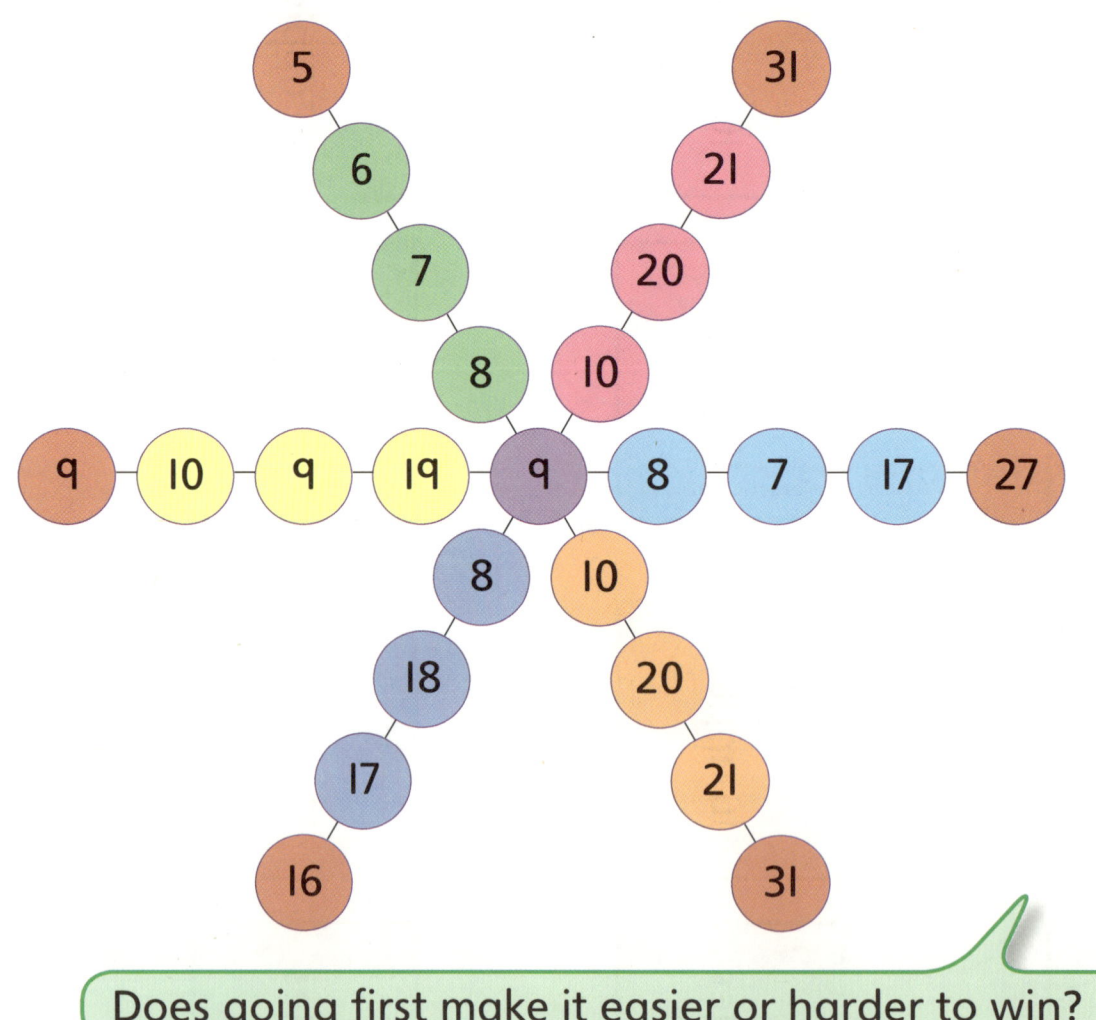

Does going first make it easier or harder to win?

 Play again, adding all the numbers you land on. Who has the highest total at the end of the game?

Four in a line

Subtraction E2

- Throw a dice.
- Put a counter on a grid number.
- Subtract the dice number from the grid number.
- If the answer is on the grid, cover it with a counter.
- Take turns until one of you gets four counters in a line.

50	49	48	47	46
45	44	43	42	41
40	39	38	37	36
35	34	33	32	31
30	29	28	27	26
25	24	23	22	21
20	19	18	17	16
15	14	13	12	11
10	9	8	7	6
5	4	3	2	1

Are there any numbers that are easier to cover than others? Why is that?

 **Play the game again. This time the winner is the first person to get five in a line.**

Counting

Fingers and toes

How many fingers are on the table?

_____

How many fingers are there in your classroom today?

Estimate: _____   Total: _____

How did you find out?

Estimate how many fingers there are in school today. How could you find out? What about toes?

Who won the race?

Place value
A3

Use these clues to find out who won the race.
Cross out each person as you answer the clue.

- The winning number does not have 3 tens and 5 units.
- The winning number does not have 6 tens and 4 units.
- The winning number does not have 1 ten and 8 units.
- The winning number does not have 9 tens and 3 units.
- The winning number does not have 2 tens and 7 units.
- The winning number does not have 4 tens and 9 units.
- The winning number does not have 8 tens and 2 units.
- The winning number does not have 5 tens and 1 unit.

How many tens does the winning number have? _____

How many units? _____

 **What is your house number? How many tens does it have? How many units? Does it have any hundreds?**

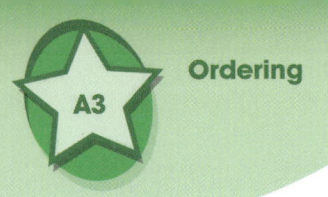 Ordering

In between

Write a number in each sandwich to make a filling number that comes in between the two numbers on the bread.

 **eXtra**

How many numbers are there between 58 and 63? Write those numbers in order. How many numbers are there between 77 and 84? Write those numbers in order.

Numbers, words and pictures

Addition B3

Match answer cards from PCM 51 to each story.
Be careful, some cards may not have the right answer!

Sarah has 6p in her purse. Her granny gives her 3p. How much money does she have in total?

Place correct answer cards here.

Jane has 12 eggs in her basket. "That's 2 boxes of 6 eggs," says Bill. Is Bill right?

Place correct answer cards here.

On day 1 Mum has an apple, a salad, some peas and a pear. On day 2 she has a carrot and a banana. Is Mum eating 5 portions of fruit and vegetables a day?

Place correct answer cards here.

There are 90 pages in this book. That's 10 times more than my favourite book.
How many pages does my favourite book have?

Place correct answer cards here.

 Make up your own question, with some correct answers and some incorrect answers. Can your partner find the correct answers?

B3 Addition

Countdown

Play this game in pairs. The aim is to get from 10 to 0.
- Put your counters on 10.
- Throw a dice and choose whether to add or subtract the dice number.
- Write a number sentence to match, such as *10 – 2 = 8*.
- Move your counter to your new position.
- Write your new number in the circle you land on.
- Take turns until someone reaches 0.

If you go too far you have to start again!

Don't go back too far! Start again.

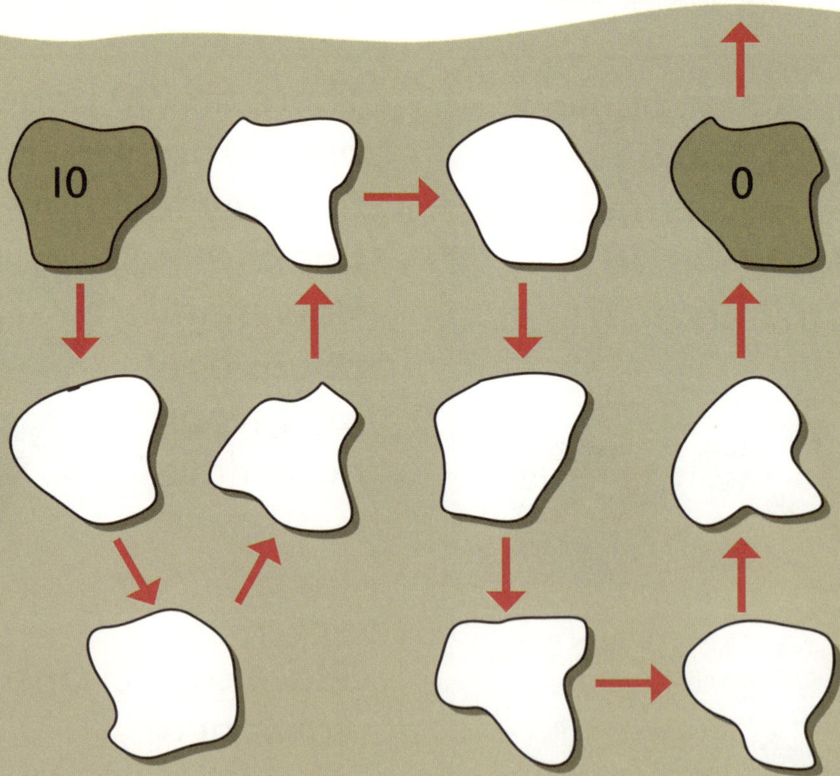

10

0

You've gone too far! Start again.

Does it matter who starts? Can you find good ways to win? Challenge another pair to play to see if you can win using what you have found.

40

Spotting ladybirds

Addition B3

This ladybird has 3 spots on one wing and 2 spots on the other. The wings have a difference of 1.

Draw spots on these ladybirds so their wings have a difference of 1. Each ladybird should not have more than 10 spots in total.

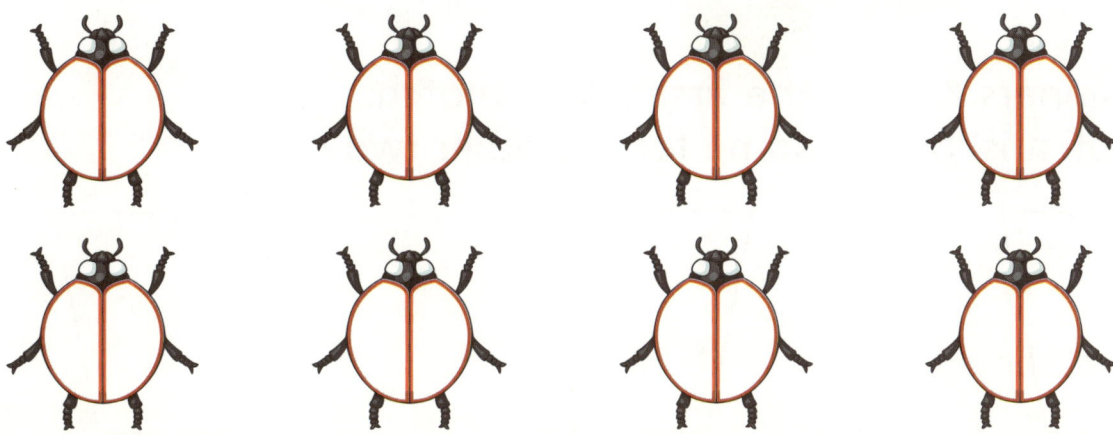

Draw spots on these ladybirds so their wings have a difference of 2.

What do you notice about the spots on your ladybirds?

eXtra Draw your own ladybirds with as many spots as you like. What is the difference between the spots on each wing?

Capacity

Spinner fun

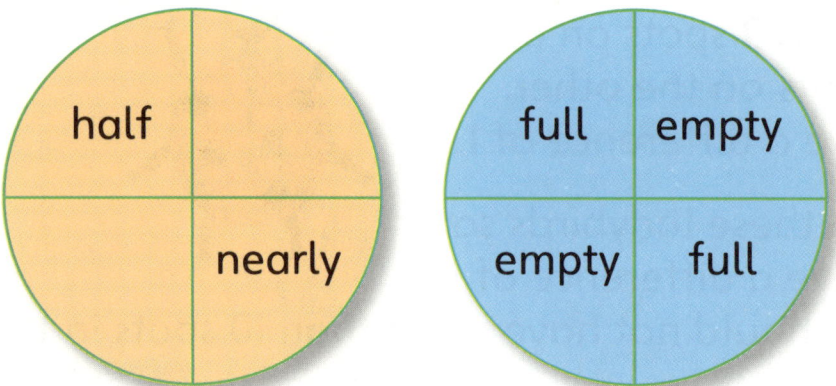

Spin both spinners. Colour the first cup to match.
Write how full it is. Do the same for the other two cups.

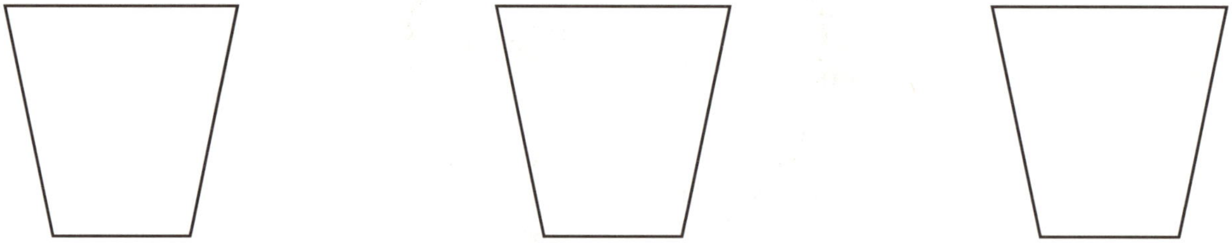

_____   _____   _____

_____   _____   _____

How many different amounts can the spinners make? ☐

How did you work it out?

Fill five different-sized containers half full of water.
Do they all contain the same amount of water? Why?

How many minutes?

Time
C3

Use a pencil and ruler to join these numbers on the clock face:
1 and 11   2 and 10   3 and 9   4 and 8   5 and 7
What do you notice about the numbers that are next to each pair?

Subtraction, addition D3

Counting

Odds and evens

| 1 | 2 | 3 | 4 | 5 | 6 | 7 | 8 | 9 | 10 | 11 | 12 | 13 | 14 | 15 | 16 | 17 | 18 | 19 | 20 |

Colour odd numbers **blue** and even numbers **red**.

How can you tell if a number is odd or even?

Take turns to throw two dice.

Add the numbers.

Is the total odd or even?

Numbers	Total	Odd or even

Is this rule always true? _____

How do you know?

_____
_____
_____

odd + even = odd

Write your own rules for adding odd and even numbers.

_____
_____
_____

Try adding next door numbers. What do you notice?